A Walk Thru

LOVE

Loving God, Loving Others

Walk Thru the Bible

BakerBooks

a division of Baker Publishing Group
Grand Rapids, Michigan

Published by Baker Books
a division of Baker Publishing Group
P.O. Box 6287, Grand Rapids, MI 49516-6287
www.bakerbooks.com

Printed in the United States of America

Library of Congress Cataloging-in-Publication Data
A walk thru love : loving God, loving others / Walk Thru the Bible.
    p.   cm. — (Walk Thru the Bible discussion guides)
Includes bibliographical references.
ISBN 978-0-8010-7181-2 (pbk.)
    1. Love—Biblical teaching. 2. Love—Religious aspects—Christianity. I. Walk Thru the Bible (Educational ministry)
BS680.L64W35 2010
241′.4—dc22   2009053578

10   11   12   13   14   15   16   7   6   5   4   3   2   1

Contents

Introduction

Sam was a model of loyalty and love. He never abandoned Frodo, even when he had every reason to do so. He chose to follow Frodo on his perilous mission to destroy the ring of power, even though hobbits always preferred the quiet life in the Shire. Along the way, Sam dove into raging waters at the risk of his own life. He singlehandedly slew the giant spiderlike Shelob that nearly killed Frodo, and then he rescued his friend from an Orc-infested tower. He thwarted an attack against Frodo by the relentlessly ring-seeking Gollum, carried Frodo up Mount Doom on his back in order to help him complete his mission, exhorted Frodo to do the right thing by dropping the ring into the fire, risked his life to pull Frodo up from the ledge of a fiery chasm, and implicitly forgave him for doing the wrong thing even as he thought both of them were dying in the fires of the mountain. He demonstrated a generous heart, a willing attitude, and a selfless spirit. He endured hardship and rejection and sacrificed himself repeatedly to prove his loyalty and assist his friend on a vital task. He did exactly what love is supposed to motivate a person to do.

At one point near the end of *The Return of the King*, the final installment in the *Lord of the Rings* trilogy, Sam and Frodo lay exhausted on the slope of Mount Doom. They had come so far in their quest to destroy the evil ring, but the last few steps of the journey seemed to be the most difficult. Frodo could go no farther. But Sam, in his determination to help, wouldn't give up. "I can't carry it for you," he told Frodo, who alone could complete the task. "But I can carry you."

That scene—in fact, that entire relationship—is a picture of what it means to love someone selflessly. Sam was willing to go to enormous lengths to do what was right for someone else. He was motivated by his affection and respect for his friend, but his love was more than a feeling. It was an inward attitude that produced outward action.

We live in a world that talks a lot about love but doesn't know exactly what it is. The word *love* is thrown around so casually and applied to so many different situations that it loses its meaning in the minds and hearts of many. And even when we do take it seriously, we don't always know how to carry it out. What is the loving response in the midst of relational conflict? When is sacrificing for someone healthy and when is it not? How do we love people who seem "unlovable"? And what exactly does it mean to love someone the way God wants us to? These aren't easy questions. That's because love isn't easy to define, it isn't easy to apply, and it isn't easy to understand.

What Is Love?

Some people think love is a feeling. Others insist that it's a decision and/or an action and doesn't involve feelings at all. The truth is that it's both. It certainly involves feelings, as in some degree of affection and emotional attachment. That's obvious in Paul's declaration that plenty of selfless actions (including feeding the poor and sacrificing oneself for others) can be done without love, in which case they mean nothing (1 Cor. 13:1–3). So love must be more than the right words and the right behavior toward someone; it has to come from the heart. But love can't *only* be an inward attitude, because it doesn't do much good unless it's expressed. For example, Scripture is clear that loving the hungry involves feeding them, and that love among brothers and sisters in Christ involves certain behaviors that demonstrate it. Love results in acts of service, words that edify and encourage, and much, much more. Love comes from within, but it works its way out.

This discussion guide won't give you a clear definition of love, primarily because the Bible doesn't give us one. No, God gives us pictures and examples and descriptions. More than that, he demonstrates love for us, especially in the person of Jesus. We'll explore how God loves us and how we are designed and called to love God, other believers, and the rest of the world. We'll see that love is central to who God is and that it's a powerful force that shapes his kingdom. And we'll see that it's vitally important for us. As C. S. Lewis once wrote, "A man's spiritual health is exactly proportional to his love for God"—and our love for God is only the beginning. Our relationship with him shapes all of our other relationships. If love is at the center of those relationships, our hearts become a lot like God's.

How to Use This Guide

The discussion guides in this series are intended to create a link between past and present, between the cultural and historical context of the Bible and real life as we experience it today. By putting ourselves as closely into biblical situations as possible, we can begin to understand how God interacted with his people in the past and, therefore, how he interacts with us today. The information in this book makes ancient Scripture relevant to twenty-first-century life as God means for us to live it.

The questions in this book are geared to do what a discussion guide should do: provoke discussion. You won't see obvious "right" answers to most of these questions. That's because biblical characters had to wrestle with deep spiritual issues and didn't have easy, black-and-white answers handed to them. They discovered God's will as he led them and revealed himself to them—the same process we go through today, though we have the added help of their experiences to inform us. Biblical characters experienced God in complex situations, and so do we. By portraying those situations realistically, we learn how to apply the Bible to our own lives. One of the best ways to do that is through in-depth discussion with other believers.

The discussion questions within each session are designed to elicit every participant's input, regardless of his or her level of preparation. Obviously, the more group members prepare by reading the biblical text and the background information in the study guide, the more they will get out of it. But even in busy weeks that afford no preparation time, everyone will be able to participate in a meaningful way.

The discussion questions also allow your group quite a bit of latitude. Some groups prefer to briefly discuss the questions in order to cover as many as possible, while others focus on only one or two of them in order to have more in-depth conversations. Since this study is designed for flexibility, feel free to adapt it according to the personality and needs of your group.

Each session ends with a hypothetical situation that relates to the passage of the week. Discussion questions are provided, but group members may also want to consider role-playing the scenario or setting up a two-team debate over one or two of the questions. These exercises often cultivate insights that wouldn't come out of a typical discussion.

Regardless of how you use this material, the biblical text will always be the ultimate authority. Your discussions may take you to many places and cover many issues, but they will have the greatest impact when they begin and end with God's Word itself. And never forget that the Spirit who inspired the Word is in on the discussion too. May he guide it—and you—wherever he wishes.

The Greatest of These

Jacob had set his heart on marrying Rachel, and he was willing to wait for her—and to work for her. The seven years he owed her father went by quickly "because of his love for her" (Gen. 29:20). Even when he was duped into marrying Rachel's older sister first, he signed up for another seven years of labor. Why? Because real love makes sacrifices, overcomes obstacles, endures hardship, and waits patiently.

While the details of that well-known Bible story are unique, the sacrificial behavior of love it portrays has been reenacted numerous times throughout history. We commonly think of sacrificial love in terms of romantic couples; however, it's the motivation of martyrs who give their lives for God, pioneer missionaries who willingly step into dangerous situations to share the gospel with strangers, parents who abandon their own dreams so their children's dreams can be realized, friends who stick with friends in a crisis, and so forth. Love can be characterized in a lot of ways, but one of its most obvious traits is its ability to move people to make great sacrifices. People with great love go to great lengths to express and satisfy it.

The Bible is the story of great love. We know how important love is because, for one thing, it's God's most celebrated core attribute. Scripture places great emphasis on love because love is what motivated God to create the world and then redeem his fallen creation. Over and over again, the Word of God encourages us to have faith, to hold on to hope, and to experience and express love. But it's clear which of these attitudes is the priority: "the greatest of these is love" (1 Cor. 13:13). That's the driving force for God and those who are made in his image.

For all the talk of love in the world—it's the dominant theme of most songs on the radio and a large percentage of movies, books, and TV shows, for example—few people actually know what love is. That's because it's hard to define. It isn't only a feeling, though it certainly involves feelings most of the time. It isn't only an action because the Bible is clear that actions without heart behind them are empty. It isn't only an internal attitude because attitudes usually don't benefit anyone but the person who has them. No, defining love is a difficult task. And if we look to the Bible for a definition, we won't find much help there either. Scripture doesn't give us a definition. It does, however, give us some profound descriptions and illustrations.

What Love Is Like: 1 Corinthians 13:4–7

First Corinthians 13 is one of the most familiar passages in Scripture, primarily because of how frequently it's read at weddings. Love is patient, kind, not jealous, not arrogant or selfish, not contentious, extremely forgiving, wholesome, and true. It "bears all things, believes all things, hopes all things, endures all things" (NKJV). And love never fails. We read such lofty words and know instantly that our own love doesn't live up to the ideal. But we also read them and realize that this is exactly what God's love is like.

As an artist keeps gazing at the details of a beautiful landscape in order to capture the scene on his canvas, we are to hold 1 Corinthians 13 before us for inspiration, encouragement, and an example to follow. This is the model we are to recreate on the canvas of our own lives. If we are not measuring our love against this standard, we will end up loving God and others in a way that falls far short of his glory.

AGAPE VS. PHILEO

The New Testament uses two words for love: *agape* and *phileo*. Many experts have long considered *agape* to be the higher form of love—unchanging, noble, and even divine. *Phileo* has been caricatured as a lesser alternative—affectionate but potentially fickle. But the New Testament use of these words isn't as clear as that. God is said to have both *agape* and *phileo* for human beings, and John is said to be the disciple Jesus loved (*agape*) in John 13:23 and the disciple Jesus loved (*phileo*) in 20:2. In fact, one could argue that because *agape* is a sometimes obligatory choice that doesn't necessarily occur in the context of a relationship, and because *phileo* involves affection that has been cultivated within a close relationship, *phileo* is a higher (or at least a more preferable) form of love. The ambiguity makes interpreting a passage like John 21:15–18 very intriguing. Jesus asks Peter three times if he loves him, using *agape* the first two times and *phileo* the third. And Peter, who declares his *phileo* love for the Lord in all three responses, is grieved by the repetition. But why? Is it because Jesus begins with the highest form of love and settles for the weakness of Peter's *phileo*? Or because Jesus begins with *agape* and has to be convinced that Peter loves him more affectionately than that?

13

Discuss

- Slowly and thoughtfully read each descriptive phrase about love in 1 Corinthians 13:4–7. Which aspects of love do you think you do well? Which ones would you most like to improve on?

  _____

  _____

  _____

  _____

- Do you think this kind of love is "doable" in any real human relationship? Why or why not?

  _____

  _____

  _____

What Love Does: John 14:15; 15:13

We know from Scripture and our own experience the great lengths to which someone will go for the sake of love. When love is on the line, people will endure painful hardship, take great risks, fight grueling battles, subdue their own desires, forgive grievous wrongs, confront when necessary, wait patiently, and always seek the good of the ones they love. Love always involves some degree of submission to the interests of the beloved—which is why Jesus told his disciples that their love for him would result in their obedience to his will. By its very nature, love gives. It moves us to surrender ourselves to the objects of our love.

The ultimate example of this surrender, of course, is giving up one's life for the sake of love. Many people have sacrificed their lives for those they are particularly attached to; Jesus did it for untold multitudes, including those who were opposed to him. Of all the ways human and divine beings can love, he said this is the greatest—the kind of love that moves someone to lay down his life for his friends.

Discuss

- Amy Carmichael, an early-twentieth-century missionary to India, said, "You can give without loving, but you cannot love without giving." Do you agree with this statement? In what sense—and to what degree—are love and sacrifice related?

_____

_____

_____

A Case Study

Imagine: Your relationship with your best friend has been a blessing to you, but over time you've noticed one persistent character flaw that not only is damaging your relationship but also undermining your friend's growth and happiness. You know that everyone has issues, including yourself, so you don't want to point a finger at your friend in an accusing way. At the same time, you truly want the best for your friend. If you confront the issue head-on, you risk losing the friendship. If you don't, you leave a potentially serious issue unaddressed.

- What's the most loving thing to do in this situation? Is it better to risk being seen as judgmental in hopes of improving your friend's life or to "live and let live"?

- What is the difference between healthy confrontation and unhealthy judgment or criticism? How do you know when a relationship is strong enough to handle this kind of honesty and when it isn't?
- If you've experienced a situation like this, what decision did you make and what was the result?

The Source of Love

Renowned theologian Karl Barth, considered by many to be the most influential Christian thinker of the twentieth century, was once asked to state the most profound theological truth he had come across in all of his years of study, reflection, and teaching. After thinking for a moment, he answered in his heavy German accent: "Jesus loves me, this I know, for the Bible tells me so."

It's a simple but profound truth. God has poured out his love on his creation through the incarnation of his Son, Jesus. This is the core message of the Bible—God's love redeeming the world from its rebellion and brokenness. That's why verses like John 3:16 are so popular: "For God so loved the world that he gave his one and only Son, that whoever believes in him shall not perish but have eternal life." Even a secular society unfamiliar with God's Word seems to know his most basic attribute: "God is love" (1 John 4:8, 16). The message is often easily distorted; many believe that if God is love, then love is God. But though the nature of divine love may not be well understood, the world recognizes the value and importance of it. Deep down in every human heart is a craving for the love of the Maker.

That doesn't mean everyone accepts God's love, of course; even longtime Christians have a hard time embracing the radical nature of his affection. "God loves you" is spoken so easily and often that we've grown numb to it. We know that God is love and that Jesus died for us, and we embrace those wonderful facts as they apply to the world in general or to other people specifically. But the nagging question inside each of us is, "Does he really love me—individually?" What's so special about that? After all, he loves *everybody*. Perhaps his love is an obligation because it's his nature to love—that is, he loves us because he has to, just as any good parent loves a child. But does he want to? Does he enjoy loving us? What we really long for is a God who is passionate for us, a God who *likes* us and is on our side. We want to know that he cares about our desires and dreams and problems and pain. That's the kind of individual connection we crave.

That's the kind of love the Bible tells us about. It's true that God's love is often described in its big-picture context, but it has many implications for each of us individually. The God whose love rescues the world also knows about each sparrow that falls and counts the hairs on our heads. And if we are ever going to know him deeply, we have to be able to experience that love. If we are ever going to become spiritually and emotionally mature, we will need to be immersed in the environment of divine love. It's how we become who we were meant to be, and it's how we are eventually able to love God back and show his love to others. Our understanding of love needs to begin with its source: God himself.

The Heart of the Holy: Exodus 34:4–7, 14

Most people don't think of Moses's dramatic encounter with God on Mount Sinai as an expression of God's love. The clouds and fire, the thundering voice, and the edicts of the Law do not evoke the warm and fuzzy feelings we often associate with love. But when God allowed his glory to pass before Moses as the prophet hid in the cleft of a rock, he declared the essence of who he is: "The Lord, the Lord, the compassionate and gracious God, slow to anger, abounding in love and faithfulness, maintaining love to thousands, and forgiving wickedness, rebellion and sin" (Exod. 34:6–7). There are frightening words in this declaration, to be sure; the holiness of God clearly comes through. But the dominant characteristics he declares for himself, even the painful ones, are all expressions of his love: compassion, grace, patience, faithfulness, and mercy. Even when declaring his righteousness, God overflows with pure and passionate love.

For millennia, Jewish theologians have seen the Sinai covenant as an engagement contract between God and his people. Though Scripture is full of images to illustrate the relationship between God and human beings—the Creator and the created, the Shepherd and his sheep, the Master and his servant, to name just a few—the most personal and powerful pictures are of the Father and his children and the Bridegroom and his bride. The one that Scripture ends with—that all of history is leading up to—is a marriage. In the theology of ancient Israel, this marriage was contracted at Sinai. It's where God revealed that he is more than a Lord and Master; he is a relentless Suitor who enters into a personal relationship with those who respond to him.

This picture becomes even clearer in God's declarations of his own jealousy (Exod. 34:14; Deut. 4:24; Zech. 8:2). He wants the worship of his people, not because he is a God of egotism but because he is a God of love. He seeks an exclusive relationship. He declares his devotion to his people, and he insists on their devotion to him in return. Those who don't understand this side of God turn his love into the shapeless sentiment so common in popular spirituality. But the biblical description of God's love is different than pop culture's definition of it. His heart beats intensely. His love is deeply personal, unrelentingly faithful, and always selfless and pure.

Discuss

- In what ways do you think popular concepts of God's love differ from the biblical revelation of his love?

  _____

  _____

  _____

  _____

- Is there any person, possession, activity, or interest in your life right now that would provoke God's jealousy? If so, how do you think he wants you to deal with it?

  _____

  _____

  _____

  _____

Persistent Love: Lamentations 3:22–23; Romans 5:6–8

"We have a God who loves. That means that we have a God who suffers," British clergyman J. B. Phillips once said. We see that clearly in Scripture as God not only allows his people to experience the consequences of sin but also suffers alongside them. He grieves their unfaithfulness and makes huge sacrifices to set things right. Through the prophet Hosea he portrayed himself as a husband who is faithful in spite of his wife's rampant unfaithfulness. Through Jesus's parable of the prodigal son, he portrayed himself as a brokenhearted father who is more than willing to accept rebellious children back into his arms. And through the cross of Jesus, he demonstrated that his love will go to excruciating lengths to make a relationship possible. As Paul wrote in Romans 5:6–8, God demonstrated his love for us even when we were completely at odds with his character, his will, and his ways. He sent his Son to die a disgraceful and painful death on our behalf. If that doesn't demonstrate the nature of his love, nothing does.

UNCONDITIONAL AND CONDITIONAL LOVE

We know from numerous Scripture passages that God's love for the world is unconditional—that is, not based on any merit or achievement of those he loves. But there's a difference between God's general love that draws people to himself and the cultivation of that love within a relationship. In some respects, God makes his love conditional on our response: "Whoever has my commands and obeys them, he is the one who loves me. He who loves me will be loved by my Father, and I too will love him and show myself to him" (John 14:21); and, "The Father himself loves you because you have loved me and have believed that I came from God" (John 16:27). Interestingly, the first of these verses uses the word *agape*—an intentional, sacrificial form of love. The second uses the word *phileo*—the kind of affectionate love common in friendship. According to Jesus's words, it seems that God has special affection for those who love him and obey him from their hearts.

God's love is patient. It endures. He doesn't get tired and give up on us. He doesn't let obstacles like our brokenness and sin stand in the way of his love. We may put up barriers or preserve distance between him and us, but he doesn't. Those who come to him will find that his compassions never fail and his faithfulness is greater than we can imagine.

Discuss

- What situations in your life or attitudes in your heart cause you to feel distant from God? According to Scripture, in what ways does God bridge that distance?

_____

_____

_____

_____

TOUGH LOVE

New Testament writers and Christian theologians throughout history have repeatedly referred to Jesus as an expression of God's love. Yet the loving Savior had extremely harsh words for religious hypocrites who opposed his ministry, calling them "whitewashed tombs" and "a brood of vipers," among other epithets. Many have wondered how the one who told us to love our enemies could have been so strident with his. One solution to this seeming contradiction is the idea that the most loving response to complacent or insensitive people who are on a course toward destruction is to confront them. Jesus's words may not have been meant as condemnation but as "tough love"—a wake-up call for those most resistant to his efforts to save them.

Extravagant Love: John 17:22–26; Romans 8:31–39

The language used to express God's love in Scripture is extravagant. In Jesus's prayer for his disciples the night before he was crucified, he declared that the Father loves his followers in the same way that he loves the Son himself (John 17:23). He concluded his prayer with a startling declaration of the purpose of his mission: "that the love you have for me may be in them and that I myself may be in them" (17:26). In other words, those who believe in Jesus are invited into the love that is shared within the Trinity. That's amazing.

Considering what we know of God, that only makes sense. We wouldn't expect an infinite heart to be limited to finite expressions of love. That's why Paul was convinced that "neither death nor life, neither angels nor demons, neither the present nor the future, nor any powers, neither height nor depth, nor anything else in all creation, will be able to separate us from the love of God that is in Christ Jesus our Lord" (Rom. 8:38–39). It's also why he prayed that Christians would be able "to grasp how wide and long and high and deep is the love of Christ, and to know this love that surpasses knowledge" (Eph. 3:18–19). And it's why John exclaimed, "How great is the love the Father has lavished on us, that we should be called children of God! And that is what we are!" (1 John 3:1). These are not subtle hints at the extravagance of God's love. They are the passionate expressions of hearts overflowing with the realization that divine love is radically deep and powerful.

Discuss

- Augustine said, "God loves you as though you were the only person in the world, and He loves everyone the way

23

He loves you." Do you really believe this? Has God's love really sunk into the core of your heart? Why or why not?

_____

_____

_____

_____

A CASE STUDY

Imagine: You and your spouse were deeply in love when you got married, and your relationship was full of hope. But hope has been put to an extreme test; after your partner's repeated unfaithfulness—sometimes flaunted in front of your eyes—the relationship seems beyond repair. Even so, you've tried to save it. You've gotten angry, given ultimatums, and poured out your heart with desperate pleas for reconciliation. At best, you receive half-hearted recommitments; more often, the response is apathy or even contempt. People have asked you why you've put up with such blatant betrayal for so long, but you've never been able to let go. Now you're starting to wonder if you should.

- How much would you be willing to sacrifice to save this relationship? How long would you hang on before you gave up?
- In what ways does the faithful partner's sacrifice and patience reflect the intensity of his or her love?
- In what ways does this situation reflect the relationship between God and the human race? In what ways is it different?

Loving God

"Who pays you to do this?" the questioners asked. "No one would risk his life like this unless he was being paid a lot of money."

The accused "criminal," a man arrested for broadcasting the message of Jesus in a country very hostile to that message, looked his accusers in the eyes and answered, "No one pays me. I do this because I love God."

This is a true dialogue from a recent interrogation, one that probably has been repeated multiple times throughout Christian history. The message of Jesus has always been contested in this world, yet many faithful witnesses have carried that message fearlessly at the risk of their own lives. Some have died with the message on their lips. Why? Not because they are paid a handsome salary or because they have a martyr complex, but because they love God. Their passion for him has become greater than their love for their own lives.

The first and greatest commandment is to love God with all our heart, soul, mind, and strength—everything. And one gets the sense that if we could obey this commandment fully, all the others would follow much more naturally. But which of us has fulfilled the greatest commandment for even a few hours? Even though God has first loved us, our love for him is often still a spiritual struggle.

Augustine said, "I would hate my own soul if I did not find it loving God." Centuries later, an Augustinian monk named Martin Luther wrote, "Love God? Sometimes I hate him!" Both knew the tension in the human soul between the love we were designed for and the love we actually experience. Coming into a relationship with God through Jesus begins to resolve that tension, but we still fall short of the greatest commandment regularly. Loving God, our ultimate purpose in life, remains our ultimate struggle.

Even so, God's love is the atmosphere of his kingdom, and our appropriate response is to breathe the atmosphere and love him in return. He knows how unbalanced the relationship is, and he has plenty of mercy for the limitations of our love. But

FAITH AND LOVE

The New Testament generally speaks of faith in Jesus as the key response for salvation. In other words, those who believe in him have come into the kingdom and those who don't remain outside of it. But Paul concludes his first letter to the Corinthians with a startling statement that makes love the central issue for salvation: "If anyone does not love the Lord—a curse be on him" (1 Cor. 16:22). And the two attitudes are closely linked in 1 Peter 1:8: "Though you have not seen him, you *love* him; and even though you do not see him now, you *believe* in him and are filled with an inexpressible and glorious joy" (emphasis added). Apparently, in the minds of these apostles, faith in Jesus and love for Jesus are two sides of the same coin.

he calls us higher anyway. His love becomes the context for our loves—all of them. Only in relationship with God can our love for him and others be cultivated.

A High Calling: Deuteronomy 6:4–5; Mark 12:29–30

The *Shema Yisrael*—"Hear, O Israel," the twice-daily prayer that begins with Deuteronomy 6:4—is considered the key declaration of Israel's faith. It begins with an emphatic statement of monotheism and continues with the greatest commandment: not only to believe in this one true God but to *love* him. In this pivotal statement, the Judeo-Christian faith distinguished itself from all other pagan gods of the time and from all competing religions since. God exists and is to be believed in and obeyed. Furthermore, he is to be loved within the context of a covenantal relationship.

Deuteronomy repeats this command several times (11:1, 13; 30:16, 20), and Jesus reiterated it as the highest in Scripture. The implication is that if we follow all of God's laws and instructions but don't love him in the process, we aren't really fulfilling his purpose for our lives. In fact, Jesus said as much to a crowd of rule-keeping religious leaders, quoting to them the words of Isaiah: "These people honor me with their lips, but their hearts are far from me" (Mark 7:6). It's possible to say all the right things and be meticulous about our righteousness but still miss the heart of God.

Discuss

- How well do you think you are able to love God? Why?
  _____
  _____

- What do you think it looks like for a person to love God wholeheartedly?

_____

_____

_____

_____

A Deep Gratitude: Luke 7:36–50

Jesus was having dinner at the home of a prominent religious leader named Simon when a woman with a sinful reputation made a scene. She stood behind Jesus, wetting his feet with her tears, wiping them with her hair, and pouring perfume on them. The foot-washing service wasn't unusual; servants often poured water over a visitor's feet and wiped them clean. But the means of this woman's kindness certainly was unique. It was emotional, messy, and awkwardly unconventional. Especially coming from a "sinner" who seemed to be intruding in Simon's home in the first place.

As Simon took a mental note of how inappropriate this interaction was, Jesus exposed his thoughts through a parable of two debtors. One debtor owed his lender a modest sum, and the other owed an impossibly enormous debt. When the lender wiped the slate clean for both debtors, which would be more grateful? Which would love the lender more? The one with the larger debt, obviously. Jesus's point was clear. Those who know how much they have been forgiven will have more love for one who forgives.

The truth is that all of us who have come into God's kingdom have experienced an enormous degree of forgiveness. But generally our love for God is proportional to how we comprehend the magnitude of his grace. When we come to him simply because we think we should, we tend to treat him casually. When we are aware that he has done miraculously great things for us, we love him deeply.

How do we express our love for him? Acts of gratitude and worship are a start. Jesus also made it clear that those who love him will obey him (John 14:15, 21). While obedience does not necessarily imply love, love necessarily implies obedience. The more we truly love God, the more we orient our lives around him.

Discuss

- What can we do to cultivate a greater love for the Lord if we aren't satisfied with the level of our love?

_____

_____

_____

_____

An Enormous Blessing: Psalm 91:14; 97:10; 116:1

In its purest form, our love for the Lord is unconditional, based not on what he has done for us nor given in hopes of what he will do for us. But that doesn't mean we can't love God "because." Scripture frequently mentions the blessings available to those who love God and promises great rewards for them. For example, God rescues, delivers, protects, and guards those who love him (Ps. 91:14; 97:10). He gives those who delight in him their heart's desires (Ps. 37:4). Some love him more because of his mercy or his willingness to hear our cries for help (Ps. 116:1). Jesus shows himself to those who love him (John 14:21), and those who love him "receive the crown of life" (James 1:12) and "inherit the kingdom" (James 2:5). None of these examples are isolated, independent, unconditional expressions of love. They are bound up in what God has already done and what he will do. That's because love is cultivated in a relationship, and relationships are built around specific experiences. They are evidence that God lovingly encounters us in real life situations.

Discuss

- Do you think loving God because of what he does is a lesser form of devotion than loving him for who he is? Why or why not?

_____

_____

_____

_____

A CASE STUDY

Imagine: You're in the middle of an extremely painful, burdensome crisis, and you've cried out to God for his help. You are trusting in his promises and—at least on good days—you truly believe he will come through for you. Then, after weeks of crying out to him, God finally provides a breakthrough in the situation, and you rejoice over his deliverance. Gratitude flows from your heart for what he has done. Your crisis is miraculously, thankfully over.

- If you've ever been in this kind of situation, how would you describe your love for God before his intervention? How would you describe it after he intervened?

- At what times is it easiest to love God? At what times do you think our love is most meaningful to him?
- In what ways can we increase our love for him before his great acts of grace are given?

Love for Others

Maria has had to put up with a lot of rejection and insults, but she doesn't mind. She knows such hostility is an inevitable part of ministering to street kids in this South American city. When she first encountered Paolo, for example, he cursed her and threatened to knife her. But what can you expect from a teenager who has had to live on the street since his parents abandoned him at the age of four? He had suffered the worst rejection a child could suffer, and it showed. The only way to break through his hardened exterior was to love him—patiently, persistently, and sacrificially. Eventually, Paolo learned to trust Maria. Then he started hanging around the shelter. Today, he's an honest, hard-working man who helps bring other kids off the street. Maria's endurance paid off.

Why does she do it? Like many people who pour out their lives ministering to others, Maria's heart had been broken by the overwhelming needs around her. She came face-to-face with the lost members of society and couldn't rest until she had done something—anything—to save at least some of them. She was more than willing to risk her safety and security on behalf of others. That's what love does. It makes sacrifices for someone else's good.

Our love for God is meant to translate into love for others. "Love of God is the root, love of our neighbor the fruit of the Tree of Life," said William Temple, archbishop of Canterbury during World War II. "Neither can exist without the other, but the one is cause and the other effect." Or, as the apostle John put it, "Since God so loved us, we also ought to love one another" (1 John 4:11). It simply isn't possible to be in a love relationship with God that does not carry over into other relationships.

A High Standard: Galatians 5:14; Mark 12:31; James 2:8

When asked which commandment was the greatest, Jesus didn't stop at just one. He began with the command to love God with our whole being, but he followed it up with a companion instruction: to love our neighbor as ourselves. This quote of Leviticus 19:18 isn't as prominent as the great commandment from Deuteronomy to love God, but Jesus paired the two. Those who say they love God must also love those whom God loves. Otherwise, they don't really share God's heart.

Paul went so far as to say that the entire law was summed up in this commandment to love others as we love ourselves. All God-given ethics for behavior are tied to this overarching truth. It's the foundation of the Golden Rule of treating others as we would have them treat us. Every "thou shalt" and "thou shalt not" related to human relationships is somehow rooted in the imperative to love one another.

Discuss

- Do you agree that it's impossible to love God without also
loving others? Why or why not?

_____

_____

_____

_____

A Divine Gift: Ephesians 5:1–2; 1 Corinthians 16:14

The command to love others isn't just a divine instruction to "be
nice." It's the necessary consequence of being made in God's
image. If God's character is to love, and we are made in his
image, it follows that we will love too. That's why Paul tells the

TRUTH AND LOVE

There is frequent tension in our lives between expressing compassion
and not compromising the truth. Much of that tension stems from our culture's perception that real love is tolerant of virtually anything in another
person's life. Scripture, however, doesn't have a problem balancing love and
truth. We are urged to speak the truth in love (Eph. 4:15), and we see clear
indications that doing so doesn't always make for a kind and comfortable
relationship. Paul, for example, rebuked a sorcerer for being "a child of
the devil and an enemy of everything that is right" (Acts 13:10)—and was
"filled with the Holy Spirit" as he spoke the words. Such an uncompromising
stance—seen also in Peter and Stephen, among others—is often the most
loving response for the fellowship as a whole or even for the individual(s)
being challenged. Loving someone does not mean accepting unacceptable
behavior. Though we often see truth and love today as being at odds with
each other, Scripture treats them as hand-in-hand companions.

Ephesians to "be imitators of God." Love isn't just a spiritual buffet item for us to choose or not; it's a vital, integral part of our original design. The God who is love fashioned us in his likeness. We aren't fully human unless we reflect his loving nature. We are to do everything in love.

What does that look like? It certainly goes beyond the world's definition of love, and it doesn't come naturally for fallen human beings. It's Jesus's kind of love: sacrificial, constant, persistent, humble, and selfless. We can't express that kind of love without first receiving a supernatural work in our hearts. Though love is a command for us to obey, it's also a gift we can't exhibit without help. It comes from God's Spirit (Gal. 5:22). We can do everything in love—in Jesus's brand of love—only by divine power.

Discuss

- In your experience, do Christians exhibit a greater kind of love than the rest of the world does? Do you think we are known by our love for others? Why or why not?

_____

_____

_____

_____

A Sacred Act: Luke 10:30–37; 1 John 3:16–18

The parable of the Good Samaritan is one of the Bible's most familiar stories. One of God's chosen people was stripped and beaten by robbers and left by the side of the road. Two religious leaders passed by and did nothing. They were probably concerned for the victim, but perhaps they didn't want to be troubled with helping him. Maybe, like many of us, they assumed that someone else could deal with the inconvenience while they went ahead with their important schedule for the day. Or maybe they didn't want to be made ritually unclean by touching what looked like a corpse. Regardless, they kept to themselves. Then a man from a despised race passed by and demonstrated true compassion at great personal cost. Which of the three passersby fulfilled the second great commandment? The third and least likely among them. The one who pleased God and conformed to God's character best was the one who actually *acted* on his compassion.

Jesus not only told stories about the kind of love he expects his followers to have. He also demonstrated it. In a sense, he played the role of the Good Samaritan. A despised, unlikely

KNOWN FOR LOVE

In explaining the expansion of the Christian movement in its first few centuries, sociologist Rodney Stark points out how revolutionary Christian love and mercy were in Greco-Roman society:

> To cities filled with the homeless and impoverished, Christianity offered charity as well as hope. To cities filled with newcomers and strangers, Christianity offered an immediate basis for attachments. To cities filled with orphans and widows, Christianity provided a new and expanded sense of family. To cities torn by violent ethnic strife, Christianity offered a new basis for social solidarity. And to cities faced with epidemics, fires, and earthquakes, Christianity offered effective nursing services.[1]

The profound sense among believers that God's love for human beings implied human beings' necessarily loving one another radically reshaped a culture.

hero, he demonstrated true compassion at great personal cost. He lay down his life for others. And this, says Scripture, is our model. According to James, true religion is serving others in need (James 1:27). The attitude of love alone is not enough; the actions of love are essential.

Discuss

- Do you think it's possible to love someone without serving them? Why or why not? Do you think it's possible to serve someone without loving them? Why or why not?

  _____

  _____

  _____

  _____

- What opportunities—including those you have taken and those you have missed—has God given you today to express love to someone?

  _____

  _____

  _____

  _____

A Case Study

Imagine: You and your friends really enjoyed worship at last week's service. The atmosphere was vibrant, the music was great, the Spirit was stirring, and one of your friends in particular seemed profoundly moved. According to his own words at the conclusion of the service, he had worshiped his heart out. But at lunch afterward, this friend was rude and demanding toward the server and, to be honest, not altogether cordial with you and your companions. In fact, his attitude after worship seemed completely self-centered.

- Why do you think it rubs most of us the wrong way to see such inconsistent attitudes between a relationship with God and peer relationships?
- Are you more likely to conclude that this friend's worship wasn't genuine, or that it was genuine but, as all of us do, he was simply struggling with some personal flaws that day? Why?
- Why doesn't our love for God always translate into love for other people? Do you think it's inevitable that someone truly immersed in God's environment of love will exude that love around other people?

Love In Christ

"Behold, how good and how pleasant it is for brothers and sisters to dwell together in unity!" (Ps. 133:1). So begins Dietrich Bonhoeffer's *Life Together*, a book on Christian community written while Bonhoeffer and colleagues were operating an underground seminary in late-1930s Germany. Bonhoeffer believed strongly in the New Testament's radical teaching that true spiritual community only exists with Jesus at the center of it—that as we find our identity fully in him, we experience what it means to be his body. And he believed that true oneness in Jesus, though a spiritual reality, was seldom truly practiced by Christians.

Most Christians realize that there's a discrepancy between the ideal of Christian unity as the New Testament presents it and the unity we actually experience in our lives. In fact, for many churches "unity" is an elusive goal. But love doesn't need to be. Even when Christians see things differently and have different agendas, love is always an option. The messy business of living and working with other Christians never precludes the possibility of genuine love. If nothing can separate us from the love of Christ, and the love of Christ is in us, then at least theoretically, nothing should be able to separate us from the love of each other.

Nevertheless, we often feel separated from one another's love. That's why it's important to remember what Bonhoeffer emphasized to his community:

> It is easily forgotten that the fellowship of Christian brothers and sisters is a gift of grace, a gift of the kingdom of God that any day may be taken from us, that the time that still separates us from utter loneliness may be brief indeed. Therefore, let them who until now have had the privilege of living a common Christian life with other Christians praise God's grace from the bottom of their hearts. Let them thank God on their knees and declare: It is grace, nothing but grace, that we are allowed to live in community with Christian brothers and sisters.[2]

A New Command: John 13:34–35; 15:12–17

Judas had already left the gathering in the upper room, and Jesus was beginning his farewell message to the disciples. It would be the last opportunity for him to instruct his friends privately. These would be important words, the key truths he wanted them to remember. So how did he begin? With a new command: "Love one another."

The command to love wasn't exactly new. The Old Testament commanded loving one's neighbor, and Jesus had already emphasized the importance of that command. But the love among his followers was to be different. The newness of this command was in how love is defined. Believers are to love each other, said Jesus, *"as I have loved you"* (13:34, emphasis added). Sacrificially. Persistently. Patiently. As deeply as the Father does. It's a lay-your-life-down kind of love.

Furthermore, this love among disciples was to be so qualitatively different from other forms of love that it could serve to validate the Christian mission. "By this all men will know that you are my disciples, if you love one another" (13:35). The clear implication is that if believers love each other the way Jesus loved, the world will know him. If we don't, they won't.

Discuss

- In what ways do you see Christians loving each other the way Jesus loves us?

_____

_____

_____

_____

NOTABLE LOVE

In extolling the "peculiarities of the Christian society," the late-second-century Christian apologist Tertullian noted how the love of Christians was an observable phenomenon to pagans. "It is mainly the deeds of a love so noble that lead many to put a brand upon us. See, they say, how they love one another, for they themselves [non-Christians] are animated by mutual hatred; how they are ready even to die for one another, for they themselves will sooner put to death."[3] Among a culture in which mercy and compassion were not seen as virtues, Christians stood out for their ability to love.

- How do you think people outside the church would perceive Christians if we loved each other as completely and sacrificially as Jesus loves us? How do you think the world would be impacted by our sense of community?

_____

_____

_____

_____

All These Virtues: Colossians 3:12–15

Compassion. Kindness. Humility. Gentleness. Patience. These are the marks of a community in which the Spirit of God is flowing freely. Of course, there are grievances and sins to forgive—no fellowship is perfect—but there is mercy to cover them all. Paul urges the Colossians to put on love over all these

"AS WE ARE ONE"

We've seen that in Jesus's high-priestly prayer in John 17, he prayed that his followers would experience the same love the Father has for the Son. But he also prayed for a further result: "that they may be one as we are one: I in them and you in me. May they be brought to complete unity" (17:22–23). In fact, Jesus prayed three times for the same oneness among believers that existed within the Trinity (17:11, 21, 22). Considering the disunity among Christians throughout history, are we to conclude that the Son had unanswered prayers? It's much more likely that Jesus was expressing a spiritual reality that is true whether we manifest it or not. Those who believe in him are bound together in his Spirit. That requires a shift in perspective: we don't seek unity as a yet-to-be-obtained goal; we seek to experience the unity we already truly have.

other virtues. This is how people with diverse backgrounds, opinions, personalities, goals, and spiritual gifts are bound together in Christ.

It's difficult enough to act out these virtues, but simply acting them out is not enough. "Love must be sincere" (Rom. 12:9). We are instructed to "be devoted to one another in brotherly love" and to honor one another above ourselves (Rom. 12:10). We must "love one another deeply, from the heart" (1 Pet. 1:22) and recognize that this kind of love is deep enough to cover a multitude of sins (1 Pet. 4:8). Again and again, Scripture urges believers to function above all else in a spirit of love—bearing with one another in the perfect bond of unity.

Discuss

- If you don't have sincere, deep-from-the-heart love for another Christian, how can you get it?

  _____

  _____

  _____

  _____

- How easily do you receive love from others? Why is receiving love difficult for some people?

  _____

  _____

  _____

  _____

- What do you think of when the New Testament speaks of the unity of believers? Does love give everyone the same plans, goals, perspectives, opinions, methods, etc.? Why or why not?

_____

_____

_____

_____

A Case Study

Imagine: Two congregations in the same city recently went through very similar circumstances. Both were growing rapidly and, as a result, needed to make some adjustments to accommodate the growth. There were opportunities for future ministries and programs; and there were challenges such as having enough space, training qualified leaders, and establishing policies appropriate for larger congregations. Within each church were several factions with varying opinions on how to address these issues. And, as is usually the case, quite a few conflicts arose as these issues were discussed and decisions were made. In one church, the conflicts eroded the unity of the congregation, created a tense atmosphere, and effectively halted its growth trend. In the other, the conflicts seemed to energize the congregation, cultivated deeper relationships among leaders and members, and in no way hindered its growth.

- Based on this limited information, what reasons would you deduce for two congregations in similar situations experiencing such different results?
- In what ways can conflict among believers be a hindrance to the gospel message? How can conflict be handled in

a way that honors the unity of the fellowship? How can unity be maintained when there's a wide diversity of goals, plans, dreams, and opinions within the fellowship?

- What do you think it would take for churches to have the kind of love that outsiders notice?

Love Outside the Family

Steve Sjogren once took a team from his church to a retail store and offered to clean the restrooms as a demonstration of God's love. The manager's shock was understandable, but her unusually harsh reaction seemed to spring from a negative attitude toward churches or Christians in general. Finally and somewhat reluctantly, she agreed to allow this act of service. As Steve and his team were leaving, she started asking questions. Eventually she opened up enough to share the pain of her past mistakes, her addictions, and the brokenness of her life—and her fear of ever coming to a church and being rejected for her flaws. Steve assured her that she and all of her brokenness would be welcome at their church anytime. His team's loving act of service had broken down a wall and enabled a skeptic to consider the love of Jesus.[4]

That's a great illustration of how the love among believers is meant to spread outside the walls of the church. God's love for the world is not just poured out *on* Christians but *through* them. Our love for each other has an evangelistic effect as people are drawn to true unity in the Spirit, but our love for those still outside the kingdom is the most powerful means of reaching them. And the bigger the challenge—the more "unlovable" someone is—the greater the demonstration of God's heart.

Human beings generally love those who are close to us and who are like us—family, friends, and social/economic/cultural peers. Christians are called to stretch far beyond those normal tendencies, even when it's uncomfortable to do so. God's mission is for the knowledge of who he is to cover the earth. The only way for that to happen is for believers to demonstrate his love in all of their relationships.

A Global Mission: John 3:16; Romans 13:8–10

"For God so loved the world . . ." It's a familiar verse that tells us a lot about God's heart, but it also tells us about our hearts. How? If we're made in the image of God and being conformed to the image of Christ, and if God loves the world passionately and sacrificially, then we will love the world passionately and sacrificially too. In fact, it's essentially impossible to fulfill the Great Commission of making disciples of all nations without having a heart of love for those nations. As Paul wrote, "Christ's love compels us" (2 Cor. 5:14). The kind of love that sees no boundaries, no races, no language barriers, no unforgivable sins, or any other obstacle is the kind of love growing in us by the Holy Spirit. Why? Because that's how God loves.

That's why Paul writes of "the continuing debt to love one another" (Rom. 13:8). It's tragic to miss opportunities to show

47

the heart of God to people who need him. Those opportunities abound—we're surrounded by people going through crises, struggling with problems, dealing with difficult circumstances, facing huge questions about life, suffering from diseases, hurting from broken relationships, and more. We may not have the solution to every problem people face, but we have the ability to love them in the midst of their problems. We are positioned as a kingdom of priests between God and a broken world (1 Pet. 2:9; Rev. 1:6). Our upward love for him will always prompt our outward love for others.

Discuss

- In what ways has God demonstrated his love toward you? In what ways do those expressions of love constitute a "debt" for you to love others?

  _____

  _____

  _____

RADICAL MERCY

As Jesus was dying, he modeled what it means to love one's enemies by praying for the forgiveness of those who were crucifying him. "They do not know what they are doing," he pleaded on their behalf (Luke 23:34). Likewise, as Stephen was breathing his last breath, he prayed for those who were stoning him. "He fell on his knees and cried out, 'Lord, do not hold this sin against them'" (Acts 7:60). In both cases, most of the enemies involved were guilty of extreme violence and hatred; and in neither case were these sins deemed unforgivable by the victims. These examples put most of our complaints against others in a humbling perspective.

- Is there any group or classification of people you have a hard time loving? If so, what can you do to overcome any mental, emotional, or spiritual barriers to showing them God's love?

_____

_____

_____

_____

Love Anyway: Matthew 5:43–47; Romans 12:14–21

Martin Luther King Jr. once said that "love is the only force capable of transforming an enemy into a friend." While that's important in any area of human relationships—whether ethnic hostilities, legal battles, conflicts at work or school, family dynamics, and so forth—it's even more so when the stakes are as high as welcoming people into the kingdom of God. As hard as it is to love an adversary, this is perhaps when God's great mercy is most clearly shown in the lives of his people. When we can love those who hate us, we are demonstrating a kind of love unknown to the rest of the world. That's why Jesus said that loving our enemies and praying for those who persecute us shows us to be children of our Father in heaven (Matt. 5:45). God rescued us while we were his adversaries (see Eph. 2:1–5), and he puts the same mission and motivation into us. If we love someone who deserves the exact opposite of our love, we are being like God.

Discuss

- How strongly are you tempted to retaliate when someone wrongs you? How difficult is it for you to let go of a

49

grudge? Why do you think letting go of offenses is hard for most people?

_____

_____

_____

_____

- What does love for an enemy look like in practical terms?

_____

_____

_____

_____

A Case Study

Imagine: You can't even remember what started it all, but for years your coworker has had it out for you. She has talked about you behind your back, frequently complained about you to your supervisor, never acknowledged your positive contributions, and tried more passive-aggressive tactics than you thought were possible. You have no idea what caused this personal grudge, but you've attempted to take the high road whenever possible. Now, through her own procrastination, your difficult coworker is neck-deep in an important project. She is struggling to handle it on her own and in danger of turning it in very late. The result if she does? A little inconvenience for the office, a lot of embarrassment for her. She hasn't asked for your help, and you know she won't. But she could definitely use it.

- How tempting would it be to let your rival suffer the uncomfortable consequences of her predicament?

- If you thought helping her would change the nature of the relationship, would you do it? Would you help her even if you doubted it would improve the relationship?
- In all honesty, what do you think would be the most loving thing to do for your coworker—show her mercy or try to let her learn a lesson?

Conclusion

Love is powerful. It can change one person's heart, and it can change the world. It can create an atmosphere of respect and honor, building up all who are touched by it. It can draw people together across social and spiritual barriers and unite them in an unbreakable bond. It can cultivate a connection between people's hearts and move them toward a common purpose that could never be accomplished alone. It can even cover a multitude of sins and bring people into the kingdom of God.

So why do we have such a hard time loving God and others? Perhaps we're absorbed in our own issues, or maybe we've been wounded in the past and don't think we can open ourselves up to such pain again. Perhaps we've discovered that loving others is difficult—it can get messy and requires persistence and hard work, more than we think we can give. Maybe we have never been taught how to love, or at least how to express it. Or maybe we just aren't convinced of what love can do in our lives and in the lives of those around us.

Regardless of our difficulties, love remains a biblical imperative. It's the one characteristic that can connect us with God's heart better than any other because, as we are told in his Word, he *is* love. When we love, we begin to understand who he is and what he is like. That alone should motivate us to grow deeper and wider in the ways we love.

Try an experiment: choose one relationship in your life to focus on, whether it's a friend or an enemy or anything in between, and then find ways to increase the love you pour into that relationship. Think of ways to demonstrate selflessness, to serve, to show appreciation, to bridge a barrier, to act kindly and compassionately, or to forgive. Closely observe the dynamics of that relationship to see the power of your love. Be sensitive to how your love is being received, but don't be discouraged by any setbacks or lack of results—real love is persistent. Over time, watch for God to work through your efforts. Then apply the same approach to another relationship, then another, and then another.

This is how lives are changed—yours and others. This is how God works through us and, even before that, how he demonstrated who he is so we could know him. In the words of an old song, "what the world needs now is love." Every one of us has an opportunity to give the world what it truly needs, just as God did for us.

Leader's Notes

Session 1

A Case Study. This situation is intentionally vague so that group members will be able to picture a real-life example from their own experience. Answers to the general questions in this case study depend on a lot of possible variables. For example, how serious is the character flaw? How open and honest has the friendship been to this point? For the sake of discussing this issue more specifically, encourage at least one or two participants to share their experience. Not only will this make for a better discussion, it may serve as valuable advice for those who are dealing with just such a relationship.

Session 2

A Case Study. This example is drawn from the life of Hosea, whom God instructed to marry a prostitute as a picture of his enduring love for unfaithful Israel. The purpose of this illustration, of course, is to demonstrate the enduring nature of God's love, not to urge spouses to remain in repeatedly adulterous relationships. That's a question for individuals and their pastors and counselors to deal with. The point is that God's faithfulness is infinitely greater than ours, and his willingness to endure our sin and deal with it is evidence of the greatness of his love for us.

Session 3

Psalm 91:14; 97:10; 116:1, discussion question. On the surface, the answer to this question may seem obvious. But if the discussion on it ends too quickly, follow up by asking whether we can even know who God is apart from what he does. Every aspect of his character revealed by the Bible is revealed in the context of his acts on behalf of somebody. Encourage participants to identify the attributes of God that are most precious to them. Inevitably, those attributes are going to be the ones they have encountered through personal experience with him.

Session 4

Ephesians 5:1–2; 1 Corinthians 16:14, discussion question. Jesus told his disciples that they would be known by their love for each other (John 13:35). If participants answer that Christians are not known primarily for our love, you may want to add a follow-up question: What are we known for? The answers to that question usually help to further highlight the ways in which we've lost our focus.

A Case Study. A good background passage for this discussion is 1 John 4:7–21, which clearly states that one can't simultaneously love God but be unloving toward others in the body of Christ (see especially verse 20). But it's also worth pointing out that a bad attitude from time to time isn't the clearest evidence of whether someone is a loving person. This case study focuses on one person's reactions on one day in order to specifically highlight the issue, but this discrepancy is really only a problem when it is observed consistently over time.

Session 5

Colossians 3:12–15, first discussion question. This is a common problem and a difficult question to answer. How do you get love for someone when you don't have it? This is where it's important to remember that while love usually involves feelings, it doesn't depend on them. It can be a choice, an act of the will. One would hope that the choice would lead to deep, heartfelt love eventually, but it doesn't have to begin there. It's also important to point out that love is a gift from God's Spirit and can be supernaturally given. Like any gift from God, we can ask for it and receive it by faith. Helpful background verses for this question include Romans 5:5 ("God has poured out his love into our hearts by the Holy Spirit, whom he has given us"); Galatians 5:22 ("The fruit of the Spirit is love . . ."); and 2 Timothy 1:7 ("God did not give us a spirit of timidity, but a spirit of power, of love and of self-discipline").

Session 6

John 3:16; Romans 13:8–10, first discussion question. This idea of a gift from God equaling a calling from God shows up specifically a couple of times in Jesus's teaching. On one occasion, when he sent his disciples out in a ministry of miracles to surrounding towns, he told them, "Freely you have received, freely give" (Matt. 10:8). Another time he told them, "With the measure you use, it will be measured to you" (Luke 6:38), a passage churches often apply to matters of financial giving but, in its original context, is specifically targeted to love-related attitudes of mercy and forgiveness. The point is that Jesus fully expected those who received the blessings of his ministry to turn around and offer them to others.

Matthew 5:43–47; Romans 12:14–21, second discussion question. This question is hard to answer in abstract terms, so in order for the group to discuss it, someone will most likely need to identify an actual "enemy" and let participants consider practical ways to demonstrate love to that person. But this can turn into a powerful object lesson if the group member(s) with the enemy is/are willing to apply some of the group's suggestions during the week and report back to the group later.

Notes

1. Rodney Stark, *The Rise of Christianity* (San Francisco: HarperSanFrancisco, 1997), p. 161.

2. Dietrich Bonhoeffer, in *A Testament to Freedom: The Essential Writings of Dietrich Bonhoeffer*, ed. Geoffrey B. Kelly and F. Burton Nelson (New York: HarperOne, 1990), p. 343.

3. Tertullian, *Apology*, accessed at http://www.earlychristianwritings.com/text/tertullian01.html.

4. Adapted from Steve Sjogren, *Changing the World Through Kindness* (Ventura, CA: Regal Books, 2005), pp. 11–13.

Helping people everywhere live God's Word

For more than three decades, Walk Thru the Bible has created discipleship materials and cultivated leadership networks that together are reaching millions of people through live seminars, print publications, audiovisual curricula, and the Internet. Known for innovative methods and high-quality resources, we serve the whole body of Christ across denominational, cultural, and national lines. Through our strong and cooperative international partnerships, we are strategically positioned to address the church's greatest need: developing mature, committed, and spiritually reproducing believers.

Walk Thru the Bible communicates the truths of God's Word in a way that makes the Bible readily accessible to anyone. We are committed to developing user-friendly resources that are Bible centered, of excellent quality, life changing for individuals, and catalytic for churches, ministries, and movements; and we are committed to maintaining our global reach through strategic partnerships while adhering to the highest levels of integrity in all we do.

Walk Thru the Bible partners with the local church worldwide to fulfill its mission, helping people "walk thru" the Bible with greater clarity and understanding. Live seminars and small group curricula are taught in over 45 languages by more than 80,000 people in more than 70 countries, and more than 100 million devotionals have been packaged into daily magazines, books, and other publications that reach over five million people each year.

Walk Thru the Bible
4201 North Peachtree Road
Atlanta, GA 30341-1207
770-458-9300
www.walkthru.org

Read the entire Bible in one year, thanks to the systematic reading plan in the bestselling **Daily Walk** *devotional.*

The **Daily Walk** devotional magazine includes book introductions, charts outlining book and chapter themes, and background information on each day's reading. Insightful observations shed light on the culture, the history, and the context of passages. Each daily reading is loaded with helpful applications that enable you to apply biblical truth to your life. Readers are sure to find the time they spend in the Bible more productive and rewarding than ever before.

Ideal for church-wide or group Bible study, bulk subscriptions to **Daily Walk** offering significant savings can be purchased online at www.walkthru.org. Discounted individual subscriptions are also available online.

WALK THRU THE BIBLE

www.walkthru.org